INSERT A PHOTO OR ULTRASOUND OF YOUR LITTLE ONE HERE.

If you don't have one, ask a sibling to draw a special photo of your baby, a shining star, or anything that reminds you of them.

Hope for the Unknown

© 2025 Jasmine Lopez. All rights reserved.
Published in Australia by Jasmine Lopez.
ISBN: 978-1-7640369-0-0

No part of this book may be reproduced, stored, or transmitted in any form or by any means—electronic, mechanical, photocopying, recording, or otherwise—without prior written permission from the publisher, except in the case of brief quotations used for review, education, or non-commercial purposes.

DEDICATED TO ALL THE BIG BROTHERS AND SISTERS
WHOSE LOVE REACHES BEYOND THE STARS.

IN LOVING MEMORY

_____

Sometimes we wonder,
sometimes we DREAM,
Life isn't always
what it may SEEM.

We hope,
WE WAIT,
we long for more,
But SOMETIMES life
won't be as before.

Waiting for baby
fills us with CHEER,
Whispering songs
they'll SOMEDAY HEAR.

Will they have curls or eyes so BRIGHT? Will they giggle, coo, or sleep through the night?

But dreams can SHIFT,
and hearts may ache.
Some things happen
we can't REMAKE.

The crib stays EMPTY,
the house is still,
A wish left waiting,
A SPACE TO FILL.

The UNKNOWN feels big, like the starry sky,

A WAVE OF WONDER DRIFTING BY.

We cry, we ache,
we question why,
Searching for answers
BEYOND THE SKY.

Some things in life,

we may not know,

But love still stays and
HELPS US
GROW.

Yet even when

the way's unclear,

GOD HOLDS US CLOSE,

His love is near.

Even if we didn't get
ONE MORE DAY,
We trust His plan,
though FAR AWAY.

Though we may stumble,

though we may weep,

GOD'S ARMS ARE STRONG,

His promises keep.

Like stars that GLOW in
the darkest night,
Hope still SHINES,
soft and bright.

Though we can't hold them,
though they're not near,
Their LOVE STAYS with us,
always clear.

And though our baby is
not here to stay,

We'll
MEET AGAIN
in a
SPECIAL WAY.

Not in our hands,

but in the sky,

A LOVE THAT SHINES

and won't say goodbye.

So trust the heavens,
TRUST IN HIS GRACE,
Even in sorrow,
LOVE FINDS its place.

"Trust in the Lord with all your heart and lean not on
your own understanding; in all your ways submit
to Him, and He will make your paths straight."

Proverbs 3:5-6

"We do not grieve like those who have no hope.
For we believe that Jesus died and rose again,
and so we believe that God will bring with Jesus
thosewho have fallen asleep in Him."

1 Thessalonians 4:13-14

"The Lord is close to the brokenhearted and saves those
who are crushed in spirit."

Psalm 34:18

"He will wipe every tear from their eyes.
There will be no more death or mourning or crying or
pain, for the old order of things has passed away."

Revelation 21:4

FOR ZION AND AMOS

In loving memory of
Ezra and Romi, so precious, so true.

This book is for you, with love shining through.
Though you're not here, your love remains,
Held in our hearts till we meet again.

A WORD FROM THE AUTHOR

Thank you for reading this book. It is an honour to share my story with you.

In 2023, I lost my son, Ezra. He was just four months old. The weight of that loss left me shattered, unable to find the words to speak. In my grief, I turned to freehand drawing, it became my way of processing emotions and hearing God's voice.

Not long after, I stepped away from the corporate world to pursue my passion for creativity. And just as I took that leap of faith, I found out I was pregnant again.
My children and I were overjoyed.

Every night, they would pray, "Please, God, don't let this baby die this time."

A week later, we lost the baby.

I was devastated. My children were, too.

They looked at me with tear-filled eyes and asked, "Why, Mum? Why again?"

And I had no words. But in the depths of that pain, I felt God's fresh wind. I spoke from my heart, and in that moment, I knew, I needed to write this book.

There are no perfect words to explain loss, but I pray this book helps you hold onto hope as you walk through the unknown with your children.

In this season of my life, God spoke to me in a way I could not ignore.
I have learned to trust Him, not because I understand His ways,
but because the unknown leaves space for faith. And in that space, there is hope.

Even when we don't have the answers, we are never alone.

Jasmine

www.ingramcontent.com/pod-product-compliance
Lightning Source LLC
Chambersburg PA
CBHW042147200426
43209CB00066B/1789